C000219085

RESURRECTION

RESURRECTION

Alister McGrath

First published in Great Britain in 2007

Society for Promoting Christian Knowledge
36 Causton Street
London SW1P 4ST

The author and publisher acknowledge with thanks permission to reproduce seven lines ('Who is third') from *The Waste Land*, taken from *Collected Poems 1909–62* by T. S. Eliot. Faber and Faber Limited.

British Library Cataloguing-in-Publication Data
A catalogue record for this book is available from the British Library

ISBN 978-0-281-05595-1

1 3 5 7 9 10 8 6 4 2

Designed and typeset by Theresa Maynard
Printed in China

contents

introduction

'Christ is risen!' This great Christian affirmation, the centrepiece of the Easter gospel, is so familiar to many of us that we rarely pause to reflect on it. The New Testament sets us alongside the disciples as they slowly and cautiously grasp the theologically impossible – that God has raised Christ from the dead in a specific place, at a specific point of history. And having accepted the impossible, they cannot stop there. For lying beyond that recognition is an uncharted sea of possibilities concerning the identity of Jesus of Nazareth, the mission of the church and the hope of the individual believer.

This book tries to create space for reflection on the meaning of Christ's resurrection for the way we think and the way we behave. It does so by engaging with some of the great themes of the biblical accounts of the resurrection, aiming to tease out their deeper meaning for both the intellect and the imagination. The New Testament witness to Christ's rising from the dead takes place at three different though related levels. In the first place, we have the reports of the totally unexpected discovery of the first Easter Day – the empty tomb. Second, we have the resurrection appearances of Christ to the disciples, which clearly persuaded them that something had taken place that lay well beyond the horizons of anything they knew. And third, especially in the letters of Paul and Peter, we find reflection on the implications of this event for our understanding of the identity of Jesus Christ and for Christian hope.

We shall be exploring some of these points in this short volume, making use of works of art to enhance the process of reflection. Yet readers will appreciate that severe limitations on space have made it difficult to engage with many of these points in any great detail. Poetry is sometimes rather more effective than theological analysis in conveying the weight and power of the great themes of this book. Consider, for example, how much theology is packed into the opening stanza of George Herbert's poem 'Easter':

> Rise heart; thy Lord is risen. Sing his praise
> Without delayes,
> Who takes thee by the hand, that thou likewise
> With him mayst rise:
> That, as his death calcined thee to dust,
> His life may make thee gold, and much more, just.

Even in the first line Herbert makes the vital connection between the resurrection of Christ and the transformation of human existence. He then moves on to develop the powerful image of the risen Christ grasping us and leading us with him to heaven. Herbert's highly compact exposition of the resurrection likens it to the fabled 'philosopher's stone', capable of transforming base metals into pure gold. The resurrection of Christ transmutes our existence from the dust of death to the gold of eternal life, and – note the neat allusion to Romans 4.24–5 – makes us righteous in the sight of God. In the same way, he implies, the dull, ordinary routine of life is utterly transfigured through the resurrection because the risen Christ holds us firmly, raising us up to where he is by his power, not by our own effort.

There is so much to explore. And the best place to begin is by considering the gospel accounts of the resurrection, pausing to read them more slowly than we otherwise might to savour their details.

Alister McGrath

the strangeness of the resurrection

Christ is risen from the dead! The resurrection message has become a settled part of the mental furniture of most Christians – something that we have come to know so well that its sheer strangeness is often lost on us. The Church's long experience of living with the message of the resurrection and experiencing its transforming impact often prevents us from realizing that it is actually an incredible, even astounding, idea. It is something that we need to approach as if we were encountering it for the very first time, appreciating just how remarkable it is.

In speaking of the resurrection, Paul uses an image that has featured prominently in Christian reflection on this great theme. The resurrection is like a seed that, having been sown, is transformed into a living plant (1 Corinthians 15. 35–38). It is a commonplace, thoroughly ordinary occurrence, seen so often that we lose sight of its extraordinariness. From a seemingly dead and dry piece of dust emerges a tender shoot. If this process did not happen, life as we know it would be utterly impossible. We would call it miraculous, were it not such a routine, everyday event. Overfamiliarity simply dulls us to the wonder of the phenomenon that we have witnessed.

Yet suppose that we were able to observe a seed going through this development for the very first time. Imagine that it might be possible to set aside our experience of the world, and instead to watch the process of sowing, germination and growth, as if we had never seen it before. Would we not be taken by surprise? Would we not appreciate burgeoning life properly for what it really is? And might not the same be true for the resurrection itself?

The need to see things afresh was one of the great themes that dominated the Romantic movement, which swept through much of western Europe and North America in the late eighteenth and early nineteenth centuries. The German Romantic poet Novalis (1772–1801) spoke of the

need 'to make the familiar strange'. The same idea was developed further by the Russian literary critic Viktor Shklovsky (1893–1984), who spoke of the importance of what he termed 'defamiliarization'. To appreciate something for what it really is, he argued, we need to be able to empty our minds and memories of all that we already know, and approach it as if it were something we had never encountered before. We should allow ourselves to be taken by surprise, to notice things that we had overlooked or seen without previously appreciating their importance.

As we prepare to consider and celebrate the central Christian affirmation of the resurrection of Christ and the hope of eternal life, we must try to imagine a world in which they are absent and unknown. We have to step into another way of thinking and living, devoid of such hope and joy. So how are we to do this? Perhaps the simplest way is to enter into the narratives of the New Testament, experiencing the darkness and pain of the crucifixion, while trying to forget the dawn that lay over the horizon. We must inhabit the experiential world of the disciples as they watch their Christ die before their eyes, without the slightest hint of divine intervention. For them, there is not even the remotest indication of heavenly concern at the death of the one they thought of as the answer to the world's ills.

The afternoon of Christ's lingering and painful death on the cross may well have witnessed the slow erosion of faith and hope in some of his followers as their world seemed to fall to pieces around them. Their hopes appeared to have been utterly and comprehensively dashed. It was as if a curtain had fallen over their Lord and their world, enveloping it in darkness. The disciples had to bury the one whom they thought should never have died in the first place. Not only did they know that he was innocent of any crime, they also seemed to have believed that he would somehow escape death altogether. The sealing of the tomb, in which the dead Christ had

been laid, was the symbol of the end of a phenomenon that might have transformed the world. Instead, it seemed to be yet another false dawn in the long history of the hopes of humanity. A sense of utter disappointment and despair pervades the gospel accounts of the burial of Christ.

On the Sunday morning, three women visited the tomb in which Christ's body had been placed with such care and devotion. The women are named: 'Mary Magdalene, and Mary the mother of James, and Salome bought spices, so that they might go and anoint him' (Mark 16.1). They would treat the corpse of their beloved Jesus with the respect and reverence to which he was entitled. (Despite the fact that the testimony of a woman was held to be of no consequence in the patriarchal Judaism of his day, Mark makes no attempt to alter the facts to make them more credible.) The three women were confronted with something they were not expecting, something that utterly confused them. Was it a trick of the early morning light? The tomb was empty.

There are many artistic depictions of this event, perhaps the most beguiling of which is Maurice Denis' *Holy Women Near the Tomb* (1894). The foreground illustrates the encounter between the three women and two angels, the eerie blue hinting at the half-light of the dawn. Jesus, they are told, is no longer here. The one who was crucified has been raised. He has gone ahead of them to Galilee.

Such are the assumptions of our age that we might expect the women to break out in spontaneous applause, perhaps puncturing the early morning stillness with whoops of joy and even the occasional 'Alleluia!' But Mark is emphatic: they are frightened, seized with terror and amazement. The vocabulary of joy is completely, conspicuously absent. The dominant tone is that of fear – a fear that reduces them to silence, and impels them to flight (Mark 16.5–8).

We might easily rationalize this alarm as fear of the unknown and the unexpected. Doubtless there is some truth in this. After all, contemporary Judaism offered a variety of understandings of resurrection, ranging from its outright denial to the hope of a future general resurrection at the end of time. Yet the idea of the resurrection of an individual in the here and now was not even regarded as a remote possibility. Nothing in their Jewish inheritance could have prepared the women for what they observed. What we now call the resurrection of Jesus did not conform to any existing Jewish expectation or belief. It was hardly surprising that the women were so frightened.

Yet this is far from being the full story. There is a deeper theme here, one that is encountered throughout the Bible. The reaction of the women is that of any human being when confronted with a revelation of the divine. We find the same fearful reverence in the account of Moses' encounter with God at the burning bush, which resulted in his commission to lead Israel out of Egypt into the Promised Land (Exodus 3.6). The shepherds in the fields around Bethlehem who witnessed the angels were likewise terrified (Luke 2.9–10): they were overwhelmed by the glory of God.

Mark's terse, direct language thus hints at the disclosure of divine glory through the discovery of the empty tomb. Although the word 'resurrection' is firmly anchored in the past event of that empty tomb, it transcends this historical landmark. Its narrative footprint upon history extends far beyond this incident as it makes an impact on individuals, changing their lives. What we term 'the resurrection' is more than an historical episode, though despite embracing and affirming this. It is about the *meaning* of that event – how it affects the way we live and think.

It is essential to note that the New Testament develops the notion of resurrection at two quite different, though related, levels. In the first place, it offers us doctrines – generalized ways of thinking, applicable to all who believe. These change how we think about life, giving us a new understanding of God, the world and our own place in the greater scheme of things. They offer us an intellectual framework by which we can make sense of things, and build our hopes for the present and the future. We find many such generalized statements in the New Testament and shall explore some of them in this book.

Yet alongside these, we find narratives of specific people, each with a unique identity and concerns, who are transformed by the resurrection. Separate, varied stories are linked to this greater story and are radically changed by it. The resurrection does indeed have a 'general' significance; yet it also has a deeply personal meaning in that it affects and transforms people in different ways. To make this point clear, the New Testament offers us powerful, compelling narratives of individual transformation, showing us how the resurrection makes an impact on single, identified people – such as Mary Magdalene, Peter, Thomas and Paul. The general and the specific are mingled, and we realize that the resurrection has the potential to illuminate and to transfigure both life and thought, respecting our individuality and distinct identity in the sight of God.

The account of the garden encounter between the risen Christ and

Mary in John's Gospel is often regarded as one of the finest pieces of theological writing of the New Testament. It tells of Mary's grief at the disappearance of the body of Christ: 'They have taken away my Lord, and I do not know where they have laid him' (John 20.13). For Mary, the body of Christ was the key to continuity with the past and her relationship with him. It was the bridge to events that mattered profoundly to her. Its absence robbed her of that vital connection.

Then Mary hears a voice speaking to her: 'Why are you weeping? For whom are you looking?' Assuming that the unknown speaker is the gardener, she asks if he knows where the body of Christ has been taken. Then the speaker utters her name. He knows it – like the good shepherd, who calls his sheep by name. And, like the sheep who in turn know his voice, Mary suddenly realizes who the man is. The Christ whom she believed to be dead has been restored to her. Awed, she addresses him as her Lord, as her 'Rabbouni' (Teacher).

This dramatic yet tender moment is captured in Denis' painting. At the centre of the work are the shadowy figures of the risen Christ and Mary, who has sunk to her knees as she recognizes the identity of her lord. There have been many artistic depictions of this scene, often referred to as *Noli me tangere* ('Do not touch me') after the next words Jesus addresses to Mary.

One of the most famous depictions of this incident is Fra Angelico's *Noli Me Tangere*, a mural painted over the period 1425–30 at the Convent of St Mark, Florence. Mary is again depicted as kneeling beside Christ in the midst of a luxurious and verdant enclosed garden. Denis retains the symbolism of this garden. Note the wall to the rear and the fencing in the foreground.

This imagery of an enclosed garden evokes the symbolism of the Song of Songs, which sets the love between Christ and individual believers in the context of a 'walled garden'. Christian theologians often saw a link between this image and the paradise of the Garden of Eden (the word 'paradise' derives from the Persian term for 'an enclosed garden' or perhaps 'a royal park'). Many theologians believe that by setting the resurrection appearance of Christ in a garden, John's Gospel is pointing to Christ's resurrection as the restoration of paradise. Access to the paradise that was lost through Adam has been regained through Jesus Christ, the 'new Adam' who brings about a reversal and transformation of the human situation.

Maurice Denis' imagery certainly points in this direction. Note especially the tree he places strategically between Christ and Mary. Early Christian writers often noted the complex symbolic relationship between the tree of life that was found in the Garden of Eden and the tree of death of Calvary. Denis depicts the tree in full leaf, perhaps inviting us to conceive of the resurrection garden as a recreated paradise, within which the tree of life is restored. No longer is humanity barred from returning to Eden. The way back has been opened, through the death and resurrection of Christ. Methodius of Olympus (died *c.* 311) makes this point. He argues that the Christian gospel makes the fruit of the tree of life available once more; those who pluck and possess it are assured of their re-entry into paradise at the resurrection.

Methodius' comments remind us that the resurrection of Christ is an event with a theoretical meaning. Yet as we have seen, it is also an event charged with a deeply personal meaning. For Mary Magdalene, it was about the restoration of a relationship and the reassurance that it could never be broken again by death. The meaning of the resurrection is existential, not just cognitive. Or, to put it in plain English, the resurrection of Christ does not merely open up fresh ways of thinking; it opens up different ways of existing and living. Life, suffering and death are seen in a new light. And the way in which we perceive things shapes the way in which we behave.

Risen Lord, help us to know you as the one who lived on this earth and rose again, so that we might rise with you and share in the joys of the paradise you have prepared for us from the foundation of the world.

the road to Emmaus

One of the most notable features of the gospel resurrection narratives is the ambivalent response on the part of the observers to what they experienced. In part, this reflects uncertainty about what they actually saw. Some saw one thing; others another. Matthew's account of the post-resurrection appearance of Christ points to the strange possibility of simultaneous recognition and 'doubting' on the part of the audience. Some fell down in worship; others were clearly bewildered by the whole thing and doubted (Matthew 28.17). Even the same person might have seen different things, as insight and recognition grew. We noted this earlier in the complex, multilayered interaction between Mary Magdalene and the mysterious 'gardener' in John's account of the post-resurrection appearance of Jesus in the garden. Mary has to 'turn' several times before she actually recognizes Jesus (John 20.11–18). We shall encounter the same pattern later in John's Gospel, in the gradual, painfully slow recognition of Jesus by the disciples after the miraculous catch of fish (see John 21.1–14).

In part, this confusion reflects one of the most distinctive aspects of the way in which human beings observe their environment. *What we see is shaped by what we expect to find.* We tend to filter our experience of the world, fitting our findings into our existing way of thinking. Observations that reinforce our expectations are emphasized and placed in the foreground of our minds; those that don't quite fit are placed in the background.

Everything we encounter in the gospel resurrection narratives conforms to this pattern. Nobody seems to have been expecting Jesus to be raised from the dead. The idea simply wasn't available to them as part of the prevailing Jewish pattern of beliefs and expectations concerning the afterlife. It wasn't part of the mental furniture that came with being a first-century Jew. The disciples who first discovered the empty tomb were clearly intending to honour Jesus' memory in much the same way as one would respect any

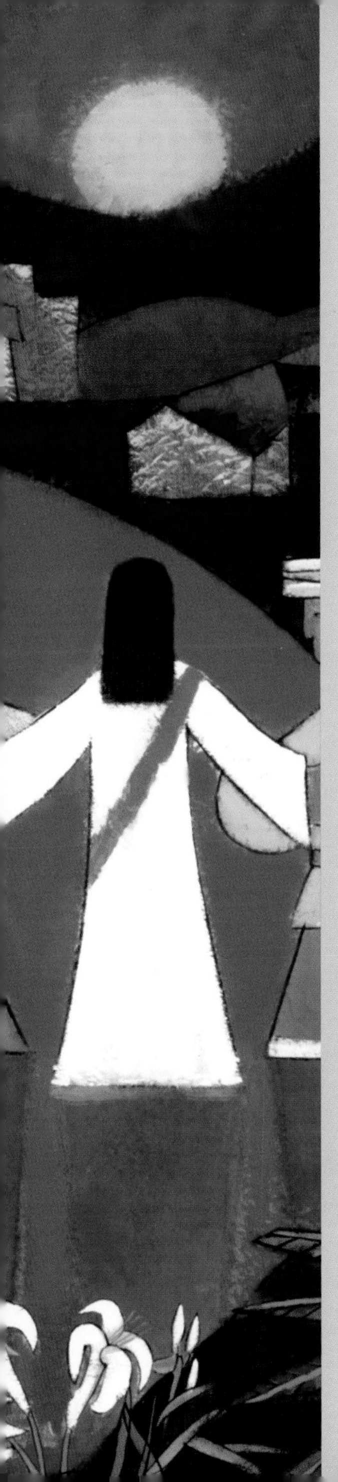

dead hero or saint. Yet they found that they were confronted with a series of observations – initially an empty tomb and subsequently encounters with Christ –that demanded an entirely new way of thinking. The evidence demanded a verdict – and traditional Jewish ways of thinking cast little, if any, light on what had happened.

None of us finds complete mental reorientation easy (as I found out for myself some years ago when making the transition from being an atheist to being a Christian). The great historian of science Thomas Kuhn (1922–96) spent much of his academic career studying 'scientific revolutions'. How, he wondered, does a major change in scientific thinking take place? Based on careful study of the history of the natural sciences, Kuhn argued that old ways of thinking were maintained until the very last minute. Then, at last, accumulation of evidence forces even the most conservative thinkers to admit that the old ideas just aren't good enough to make sense of new evidence. A 'paradigm shift' is required to understand.

A similar process can be seen happening at places in the New Testament. The gospel accounts of Christ's resurrection appearances show us a paradigm shift taking place within the first community of Christians. Some are wedded to the traditional beliefs of Judaism. Resurrection only happens on the last day! So Jesus simply cannot have been raised from the dead. The theory doesn't allow it. There must be some other explanation – mustn't there? Their bewilderment is partly due to their growing realization that something has happened that simply does not fit the settled assumptions of their world. Others grasp the reality of the situation more quickly, realizing what must have happened and beginning to appreciate its significance.

By the time of Paul's letters, the tectonic plates of existing ways of thinking about God, humanity and Jesus of Nazareth have undergone a massive change. One of the most important aspects of this seismic shift

He Qi 1997.

has to do with the identity of Jesus and his relationship with God – themes that we explored in *Incarnation*, another volume in this series. What, many scholars rightly ask, could have precipitated such a huge revision of existing understandings of the identity of Jesus of Nazareth? For many, only one answer is adequate: something unexpected took place that forced such a radical review. The resurrection fits that particular bill perfectly.

At several points, we can see this process of transition actually taking place within the narratives of the Gospels. This pattern occurs in one of the most famous road narratives of the New Testament – the story of the road to Emmaus, related only in Luke's Gospel. The narrative takes place on the afternoon of the first Easter Day. Two followers of Jesus of Nazareth are walking towards the village of Emmaus, discussing the recent events in Jerusalem. We know nothing about these two characters, save that one is named Cleopas. (We might speculate that the other is Mary, who is identified as the wife of 'Clopas' elsewhere: John 19.25). As they walk the seven miles to the village, they are joined by a stranger, who asks what they have been talking about. They do not recognize him.

As they explain the topic of their discussion, we can see the tensions building up in the tectonic plates of their world-views. The ageing wineskins cannot cope with the new wine and are on the point of bursting. The old is about to give way to the new. They have, they tell their travelling companion, been talking about Jesus, who was 'a prophet mighty in deed and word before God and all the people' (Luke 24.19). They had 'hoped that he was the one to redeem Israel' (24.21). We see here an understanding of Jesus that places him firmly within the characteristic ways of thinking of first-century Judaism.

First, Jesus is described as a 'prophet' – an accepted existing Jewish category that may have helped to make a little sense of Christ's identity. In the end, though, it restricted that understanding because it limited Jesus to existing Jewish ways of conceiving God's mode of operation in the world.

Second, the two disciples hoped that Jesus was 'the one to redeem Israel', again drawing on existing Jewish Messianic expectations. The dream of one who would liberate Israel went back to the time of the Exodus, and remained a potent vision as Israel was occupied by various foreign powers. There was a strong expectation that, when Gentile oppression was at its height, the God of Israel would again step in to deliver Israel, using human agency to achieve this divine goal.

The two disciples, though they may not have known it, were on the brink of a breakthrough. They were about to find out that Jesus was something far greater than existing Jewish categories suggested or permitted. A fault was developing within the tectonic plates. Sooner or later, there would be a major shift. The old structures would shudder and crumble, making way for the new. The old wineskin was about to be burst by the new wine. The conversation with the mysterious stranger proved to be the catalyst for this transition. The old way of looking at things would have to be abandoned. On this traditional model, the crucifixion of Jesus could be interpreted only as a failure. The mission of Jesus of Nazareth – like that of other recently failed claimants to the title of 'Messiah' – had ended in utter defeat and failure, leaving Israel where it had been before.

We are told that the stranger speaks to the two disciples: 'Beginning with Moses and all the prophets, he interpreted to them the things about himself in all the scriptures' (Luke 24.27). He relates the *full* story, offering a new way of reading it, and making sense of Israel's history. And, above all, he offers a new way of locating and interpreting a vital part of that great narrative – the story of Jesus himself. This is not about another failed Messianic uprising, routed by the Romans. It is about a new era in the history of God's dealings with his people and with the world, in which suffering and death will be confronted head on and defeated. 'Was it not necessary that the Messiah should suffer these things and then enter into his glory?' They had been trying to unlock the meaning of recent history with the wrong key. And as they walk along the dusty road, a new key is slowly but surely placed in their hands and turned in the lock. And the door opens to a new way of understanding.

This incident is the topic of a striking picture by one of China's most important Christian artists, He Qi. The ending of the Cultural Revolution in the People's Republic of China witnessed two important developments: the re-emergence of an interest in all forms of art and a rebirth of Christianity. Perhaps it was inevitable that these two powerful streams should converge, leading to a renaissance of Christian art, with He Qi emerging as one of its leading proponents. He Qi's interest in Christianity arose partly through encountering Raphael's *Madonna and Child* in the early 1970s. At that time, he was churning out portraits of Mao Zedong to meet the needs of the Communist Party. Yet Raphael's masterpiece spoke to him of a personal peace that he had not encountered elsewhere. Sensitive to the criticism that Christianity was a Western import into Asia, He Qi attempted to develop an authentically Chinese approach to Christian art. He held that the doctrine

of the incarnation provided the theological basis for 'the indigenization of Christian art in China'.

He Qi's vivid depiction of the road to Emmaus sets us behind the three characters as they walk along the road, the sun setting in the sky ahead of them. There is no hint of a reverential attitude on the part of the two disciples. They have not yet discerned the identity of the one who is with them. He is a fellow traveller, sharing in both their physical journey on the road and their mental struggles to make sense of what has happened at Jerusalem. As the day draws to its close, they ask their new friend to stay and share a meal with them. Yet it is not what Jesus has said, but what he does, that changes their perceptions. 'When he was at the table with them, he took bread, blessed and broke it, and gave it to them. Then their eyes were opened, and they recognized him' (Luke 24.30–31). We see here once more the central paradox of the gospel resurrection accounts. The disciples really meet Jesus, as he always was, a person of flesh and blood. Yet at first they do not recognize him. And when they do, they recognize that he is something more than mere flesh and blood.

And with that recognition comes a complete reconsideration of the 'big picture' – the story of God's dealings with his people. A new way of understanding the nature of that story, and especially Jesus' place within it, emerges. 'Were not our hearts burning within us while he was talking to us on the road, while he was opening the scriptures to us?'

Luke's account of this incident is compressed, even terse at points. Yet its main themes are clear. A personal encounter with the risen Christ utterly altered the landmarks of the two disciples' world. Once they realized that the figure who walked and talked with them was the Jesus whom they were invited to recall in the breaking of the bread, they could no longer think of him as a dead martyr or prophet.

The story of the mysterious, transformative encounter on the road to Emmaus has always exercised a potent appeal to the poetic imagination. It is alluded to in T. S. Eliot's early masterpiece *The Waste Land* (1922), where it is linked with the imagery of an Antarctic expedition. Eliot was intrigued by a report, possibly concerning Ernest Shackleton's expedition of 1914–16, that 'the party of explorers, at the extremity of their strength, had the constant delusion that there was one more member than could actually be counted'.

> Who is the other who always walks beside you?
> When I count, there are only you and I together
> But when I look ahead up the white road
> There is always another one walking beside you
> Gliding wrapt in a brown mantle, hooded
> I do not know whether a man or a woman
> – But who is that on the other side of you?

Eliot clearly saw a significant parallel between the experience of these exhausted Antarctic explorers on the 'white road' and humanity's journey through the barren wasteland of life. Although Eliot makes clear that he has in mind the 'moral decay of eastern Europe' in the aftermath of the Great War, his line of thought is easily transposed to an aggressively secular world from which God has been excluded; a God who, nevertheless, dogs our steps, unwilling to let us go. In South: A Memoir of the Endurance Voyage, Shackleton wrote of his experience on that expedition:

> When I look back at those days, I do not doubt that Providence guided us, not only across those snowfields, but also across the stormy-white sea which separated Elephant Island from our landing place on South Georgia. I know that during that long march of thirty-six hours over the unnamed mountains and glaciers of South Georgia it often seemed to me that we were four, not three.

For Eliot, the narrative of the journey to Emmaus illuminated the predicament of his own generation. In his eyes, it was a generation that believed it travelled alone, without God, yet which constantly discovered the presence and action of someone who was not supposed to be there, who was not relevant.

Lord, help us to discern you as you accompany us through life. May we know you through the reading of Scripture and the breaking of bread, and may our hearts burn within us as we encounter you.

too good to be true?

Christianity is a religion that is grounded in history, which is one of its greatest strengths. Why is this point so important? Part of the answer lies in the simple fact that each of us lives in history – it is where we find ourselves. It is as much part of being human as breathing air and drinking water. And the Christian faith speaks of a God who acted in history, not one who is detached from it. God enters into our homeland in order to bring us to the new homeland that awaits us. To encounter God, and to be transformed by that encounter, we do not need to escape from history. He graciously and generously comes to meet us where we are, rather than demanding that we meet him where he is.

Part of the gospel of grace is that God has entered into human history in human form, to live in our world. This divine inhabitation – or 'incarnation' – of our world focuses on the slice of the past that we know as the story of Jesus of Nazareth. Although specific to one era and place – the land of Palestine two thousand years ago – what happened there and then has the capacity to transform the here and now. As we shall see, one significant aspect of the resurrection is its abolition of any historical limitation on the risen Christ, who is able to meet people at any place and any time.

Yet this strength might be seen as a weakness. How can we be sure about what happened long, long ago and far, far away? We weren't there. We can't be absolutely sure about the precise historical events – and neither could anyone at the time. The finest historical study will simply bring us to the point where we can offer only the 'best explanation'. That is, the tomb, which previously contained a thoroughly dead and professionally executed Jesus, was empty; and that his followers saw and encountered someone they were convinced was this same Jesus – physically alive but in a new, transformed way.

History does not deal in certainties, as the furious historical debates about even recent events make clear. But we can speak with complete integrity about the 'best explanation' of the historical observations. The type of reasoning that historians characteristically employ in exploring the past (for example, the 'best explanation' is tested rigorously in terms of its additional capacity to explain other developments) points strongly towards the bodily resurrection of Jesus. But it cannot prove, nor can it be, the basis of faith. There will always be those who, holding fast to the dogmas of their age, say something like this: 'I can't think of a better explanation at the moment. But there has to be one somewhere, because I know that the resurrection can't have happened.'

So why did this new, problematic belief in the resurrection of Christ gain such wide and rapid acceptance? In the end, we shall never fully understand how the first Christians came to grasp what had happened and explain its significance. Yet the New Testament, both in terms of what it tells us and (perhaps even more intriguingly) does *not* tell us, points to the quick assimilation of this idea and its implications being equally speedily explored.

The New Testament witness implicitly points to the initial assumption on the part of Jesus' close circle that his ministry had been abruptly and permanently terminated by the crucifixion. After his death, it seems that those close to Jesus intended to venerate his tomb, a long-standing Jewish custom widely held to be an appropriate mark of respect for the dead. Yet these plans were thrown into complete confusion by the disconcerting discovery that the tomb was empty.

The New Testament, along with all known early Christian documents, is silent at those points where we might expect to find rebuttals of alternative explanations of the 'resurrection'. We often overlook the simple, yet enormously significant, point that the rapidly spreading accounts of Jesus' resurrection could have been stopped dead in their tracks by producing and

publicly displaying his corpse. However, there is not even a hint in any known historical documentation that the Church was obliged to explain away the dead body of its supposedly resurrected Lord.

The contrast with earlier periods and figures in Jewish history is worth noting. Other Jews had died after promising that they would be raised from the dead. One particularly obvious example is provided by the Maccabees, who rebelled against the pagan invaders of the land of Israel two centuries before Christ. Their followers regarded them as national heroes and righteous martyrs, believing passionately that they would be raised from the dead. Yet no widespread belief in resurrection arose around this time. There were no claims about the resurrection of the Maccabees in general or, indeed, of any individual Maccabee. There was nothing to report, nothing to interpret. The case of Jesus of Nazareth was utterly different in this respect. Something extraordinary had clearly happened and demanded explanation. The early debates recorded in the New Testament between Christians and their Jewish critics centred on the interpretation of the resurrection. What did it *mean*?

In answering that question, the first Christians found they had to walk into unmapped territory, away from the safe, well-known places of traditional Jewish religion and beliefs. They had to move into places so familiar to us that we forget they were once very strange indeed. Yet familiarity does not make something right or true. At this point, we encounter one of the commonest of the arguments directed against the Christian faith, especially its belief in resurrection. We Christians are told it's just something that we have invented because we would like it to be true. 'You believe what you want to.' This cynical judgement of our culture must not be lightly dismissed. Many would argue that we decide what we would like to be true, and then make the evidence fit that belief. Faith is a dreamworld we conjure up to console us in moments of vulnerability, hoping it will shield us from the darker truths of life.

It is a radical thought. In fact, it is so radical that it is rarely followed through with anything like the logical rigour it deserves. For an argument originally devised by early nineteenth-century critics of religion (such as Ludwig Feuerbach and Karl Marx), to counter its claims actually has the capacity to undermine all world-views, including atheism. Whether Christian or Marxist, religious or secular, all world-views ultimately rest on faith. They cannot prove their central ideas with certainty. Most of us are aware that we hold many beliefs that we cannot prove to be true but nevertheless think are perfectly reasonable and defensible. At some point, we have to make an imaginative leap from what is definitely known to what we believe to be true. We do it all the time, often without realizing that we are.

Atheism itself is vulnerable to precisely this kind of criticism. Sigmund Freud, the father of psychoanalysis, was quick to argue that believing in God was an illusion grounded in human longing for consolation. Even so, he had little time for the disturbing thought that atheism might be equally illusory, grounded in the human longing for autonomy. One of the driving impulses that brought the modern world into existence was the human desire to be free – free to make our own choices, choose our own destinies and not be accountable to any higher authority for our decisions.

This point is made by the Polish writer Czeslaw Milosz, who won the Nobel Prize in Literature in 1980. Karl Marx had argued that religion was the 'opium of the people'. Milosz riposted by pointing out that today's opium of the people was the belief that we were responsible to no one, and would never be held to account for what we did. Believing that there is no God is just one aspect of the human yearning to do what we like, be whom we choose and be subject to nobody.

'You believe what you like' may well be the wisdom of our day, but it is a double-edged sword, wounding those who use it as much as those against whom it is used. Yet it forces Christians to examine their faith and ask the initially threatening yet ultimately helpful question: '*Why* do we believe in the resurrection of Christ?' Some Christians regard it as disloyal or irresponsible to ask such questions, fearing that it calls the authority of the Church or their favoured Christian writers into question. Yet in reality this is not the case. The real issue here is the need to explore our faith, refusing to rest content with a superficial acquaintance with its ideas and wanting to go deeper.

The human need for reassurance is as profound as it is understandable. We want to be able to check things out. We want to know that we have not chosen to build our lives on a fiction, delusions or lies, even though they might be 'lies breathed through silver' (C. S. Lewis). Let's look briefly at some points before moving on to consider a famous incident in the gospel accounts of the resurrection.

Precisely because we have got so used to the 'good news of the resurrection', we tend to assume that Jesus' rising from the dead would be universally considered a sign of hope. Yet the evidence suggests that many would have seen this as something deeply troubling, even grotesque.

The idea of the dead returning to the land of the living was seen as very threatening, especially in Roman pagan thought. The dead were safely confined to a shadowy world and could never return. The realization that Jesus had broken free from the bonds of death would have caused terror and amazement in about equal measure. And that is exactly how the Gospels portray initial reactions to this declaration. It was not an easy idea to accept; for most, the return of the dead to haunt the living would not be an attractive idea. The Roman state would be in serious trouble if the many rebels and revolutionaries it had executed returned from the dead to stir up fresh dissent.

As we have seen, even within the broad spectrum of views on the afterlife that jostled each other in the first-century Jewish context, no one expected human beings to be resurrected in the here and now. Resurrection was at best a vague hope for the distant future, when God would finally raise all people at the end of time. Some groups within Judaism (such as the Sadducees) altogether denied this idea. (Paul, it will be remembered, was able to exploit these differences between Jewish religious parties when the occasion demanded: Acts 23.6–8).

The account of 'Doubting Thomas' illustrates this early ambivalence, even within Jesus' immediate circle, about a resurrection taking place in the middle of history. The gospels tell us frustratingly little about Thomas, recording few statements directly attributed to him. He comes across as a hard-nosed realist, tinged with a world-weary pessimism. Like the others around Jesus in the final days of his ministry, Thomas was traumatized by his Lord's execution. Unable to cope with that dreadful incident and its possibly more dreadful implications, he slipped away from the others at the very time when everything began to change. As a result, he knew nothing of the resurrection appearances that so transformed the outlook of the other apostles. On hearing their accounts of this astounding event, he simply refused to believe them.

Why? Many answers can be given. The most obvious is that Thomas regarded these reports as incredible. He wanted proof before he would commit himself. Yet other factors may also have been involved here. Was Thomas conscious of having become an outsider, set apart from the others through not having shared their experience of the risen Christ? Yet whatever the explanation for his doubts and hesitations, it was clear that Thomas wanted reassurance: 'Unless I see the mark of the nails in his hands, and put my finger in the mark of the nails and my hand in his side, I will not believe' (John 20.25). Many of us, in our heart of hearts, know that we would have done the same. Thomas is a representative figure who brings our doubts and hesitations into the open.

The encounter that follows is both moving and transformative. The risen Christ greets Thomas as one whom he knows and loves, whose secret fears and doubts are already laid open to him as if they were written in a book. The scene is depicted with great care and insight by Guercino (1591–1666), whose *The Incredulity of St Thomas* was executed in 1621 for

Bartolomeo Fabri. The risen Christ stands among the disciples, bearing the victorious banner of resurrection. This is not a disembodied spirit, wraith or ghost. Christ has been raised bodily – as one who can be recognized, even by Thomas. Graciously and gently, without any hint of sarcasm or anger, the risen Christ invites Thomas to see for himself, to touch, to explore, to confirm: 'Do not doubt but believe' (John 20.27). (The text, it should be noted, gives no hint that Thomas actually put his hands in the wounds. Guercino has exercised a little artistic licence here, following a long tradition.) It is enough. Thomas responds with an affirmation of faith, mingling personal trust with theological insight: 'My Lord and my God!'

Yet Christ's response needs to be noted. Thomas, he gently hints, may have had it easy. He was able to have his doubts resolved, there and then. There would be others in the future who might have the same doubts but who can never hope to have them so comprehensively and convincingly dispelled. 'Blessed are those who have not seen and yet have come to believe.' Those words are spoken to us. And we need to hear them.

Lord, help us to trust that you are risen and stand alongside us in our journey of faith.

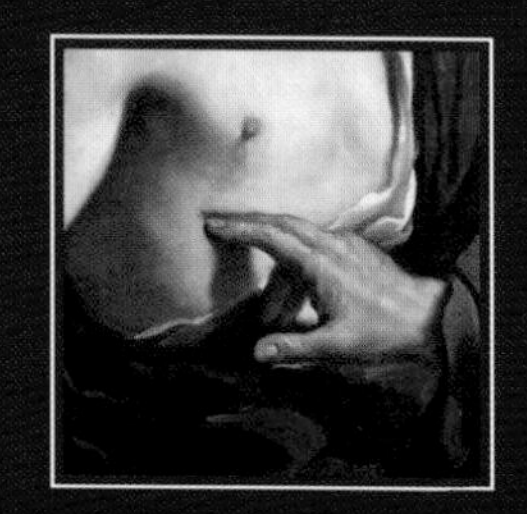

the transfiguration of a failure

4 the transfiguration of a failure

The resurrection of Christ appears to have taken the first Christians by surprise. We might gently chide them for their failure to grasp what had happened, if we forget that we have benefit of hindsight. It's easy to get things right when you already know the answers. We look back on what happened from the standpoint of those who know and (at least partly) understand. They, on the other hand, encountered the resurrection at first hand in all its astonishing, bewildering novelty.

The importance of this point is too easily overlooked. Well-meaning preachers (and I include myself in their number) often take theological short cuts, weaving themes found elsewhere in the New Testament into the gospel narratives of the empty tomb and resurrection appearances of Christ. We often tell our congregations that the message of these narratives is simple: Jesus has been raised from the dead! And that means that we shall also be raised up on the last day! This conclusion is true, yet this is *not* what the resurrection narratives actually say. If we empty our minds of the theology of the resurrection that we find in Paul's letters and elsewhere, we are confronted with a series of rich, highly symbolic, intellectually profound events, all of which demand careful reflection.

One of the most astonishing features about the resurrection narratives is that at no point does Jesus or anyone else mention the future hope for believers – neither in terms of the hope of heaven or salvation, nor, indeed, of resurrection itself. All that still has to be worked out. This hope may indeed be implicit in what has been said, lying just beneath the surface of events, waiting to be affirmed and explored. But it is not stated openly: it is the fact, the actuality, of the resurrection that is the prime concern at this stage. Reflection does follow; at this stage, however, that has yet to happen. Keys are beginning to turn in the locks of the mind, but the doors have not yet opened fully to the resurrection gospel's new wine.

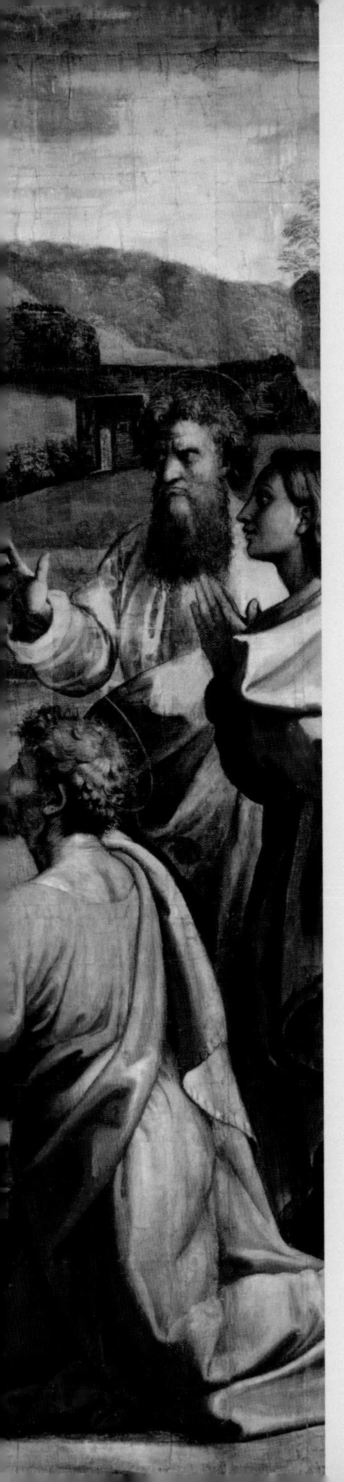

By reading the Gospels closely and attentively, we can grasp something of the life-changing astonishment that the events created within the circle of those first Christians. Their minds and imaginations were forced to expand and their horizons to be raised while they tried to take in the magnitude of this undeniable and great new work of God. As we have seen, Mary Magdalene and Thomas the Twin were transformed in their ways of thinking and their outlooks on life. But what about the other disciples? What, for example, about Peter?

In subtly different ways, the four Gospels portray Peter as the leader of the first Christians, the spokesperson for the disciples as they followed Jesus of Nazareth and tried to make sense of his identity and significance. In the aftermath of the resurrection, the disciples looked to Peter as the era of the Christian Church dawned. So how did Christ's rising from the dead make an impact on his personal world?

As a historian, I have often noticed how new religious and political movements often try to portray their chief figures in the best possible light. The failings and weaknesses that are so characteristic of human nature are often airbrushed out of the picture. Yet the Gospels portray Peter as a thoroughly human character, with reassuringly human strengths and weaknesses. This is perhaps most clearly seen in the moving account of Peter's failure in the courtyard of the High Priest in Jerusalem. After the Last Supper, as Jesus walked towards the Mount of Olives with his disciples, he spoke to them darkly about what was about to happen. They would all abandon him (Mark 14.27–28). There was no trace of anger in his words. He was simply telling them what the future held.

Peter, however, was outraged at such a suggestion. Others among the disciples might desert Jesus (did he look around him, accusingly, at this point?) – but *he* would never, ever do such a thing. Nobody could doubt

Peter's commitment to his Lord, nor his belief that, when the going got tough, he would rise to this challenge. Yet Jesus knew otherwise. The spirit might be willing; the flesh, however, was weak. How many aspirations have been shattered through a failure to be realistic about the limitations of human nature?

Gently, kindly, Jesus explained that Peter hardly knew himself or the challenges he would face. Peter would deny Jesus, not merely once, but three times before the cock crowed twice. (The reference here is probably to the Roman military trumpet call sounded during the night to mark the beginning of the fourth watch at 3 a.m.) It was a thought that Peter could not bear: even if he had to die for doing so, he would never deny Jesus (Mark 14.29–31).

We shake our heads wisely as we read these words, knowing how things will actually work out. Yet Peter deserves to be understood here rather than censured. His motives were bold and true. What he had yet to confront was the weakness of his own nature which, when put to the test, failed him. After the arrest of Christ, Peter stood in the courtyard of the High Priest, warming his hands over a charcoal fire. His first challenge came from someone who could hardly be regarded as a powerful, dangerous opponent – a servant girl: 'Weren't you one of those with Jesus, the man from Nazareth?' Her question probably arose from nothing more than idle curiosity. Yet even this innocent question proved too much for Peter. He vigorously denied any knowledge of Jesus.

Perhaps he protested too much. The servant girl wasn't satisfied with his answer. She turned to those standing around, expecting them to back her judgement; she eventually got some support from within the crowd. Clearly frightened, Peter twice more denied having any knowledge of Christ. At that point, the 'cock crowed for the second time'. Peter then realized what he had done. Not only had he failed Jesus, he had failed himself. He was humiliated in his own eyes. Little wonder that he broke down and wept (Mark 14.66–72). His situation seemed irredeemable.

Many of us have found ourselves in similar dark places. Our eyes need to be opened to our weaknesses and flaws. Why do so many find that a spectacular failure is often the gateway to personal transformation and renewal? One answer might be that it forces us to be honest about ourselves, destroying our comforting illusions about our nobility and integrity. Failure holds up a mirror and invites us to see ourselves as we really are. It forces us to be honest and to start all over again.

Yet in Peter's case, the situation seemed to lie beyond redemption. With the death of Christ the following day, the world was a grim and bleak place. Jesus was dead, and the chief of his disciples was a failure and a coward. There was nothing to alleviate the unremitting gloom of the moment. The most that Peter could do was show his respect for his dead Lord by visiting his tomb. Then came the astonishing events of that Easter morning . . .

The full significance of the resurrection for Peter's personal situation is explored in a remarkable passage in John's Gospel. The passage tells of how the risen Christ encountered Peter and the disciples by the shores of 'the Sea of Tiberias' (otherwise known as Lake Galilee). The disciples had drifted back to their former occupations, including fishing, waiting to be told what to do. On this occasion, they fished all night but caught nothing. They were then joined by a stranger, who invited them to cast their net to the right-hand side of the boat. Suddenly, it was full of fish.

It was as if history were repeating itself. The events that led to the original calling of the disciples three years earlier were being repeated (see Luke 5.2–10). Christ met them once more by a lake as they were fishing, and everything changed. Their eyes were opened and they recognized the stranger. We see here a significant point, that is often overlooked – the importance of *action* in disclosing Jesus. Here, it was an action that invoked the memory of the calling of the disciples – the sharing of bread and fish by the seashore. The one who originally called them was present once more, and was now calling them to new tasks and challenges. In the case of Cleopas and his colleague, the action of breaking bread after the walk to Emmaus finally opened their eyes to the identity of their mysterious travelling companion.

The gospel narrative on this occasion focuses on the figure of Peter, who is confronted with more symbols of his past before being commissioned for the future. Christ meets with Peter on the shore of the lake. He is standing by a fire on which some fish are cooking. Nearby, there is some bread. The bread and fish immediately call to mind the great miracle of the feeding of the five thousand – a sign of the authority of Christ over nature, and his compassion for his people. Yet it is the fire that has especial importance as a symbol of past failure. For it was by such a fire in the courtyard of the High Priest that Peter denied Jesus three times. Each of these denials is about to be confronted, so that each may be forgiven and transfigured. Three times Christ asks Peter substantially the same question: 'Do you love me?' Puzzled, and not a little hurt, Peter eagerly affirms his

unconditional love for his risen Lord. In return, he receives a commission: to feed and care for Christ's sheep.

The scene has been an inspiration to countless artists, not least to Raphael (1483–1520). In 1515, Pope Leo X invited Raphael to submit ten designs, based on the lives of Peter and Paul, for great tapestries that would adorn the walls of the Sistine Chapel in Rome. Raphael duly submitted ten 'cartoons' of his ideas, which were forwarded to the greatest tapestry centre of the age – the Brussels workshop of the weaver Pieter van Aelst. In 1623, the English monarch Charles I purchased seven of these cartoons, intending to use them to inject life into the struggling English tapestry industry. They remained the property of the British royal family, and in 1865 passed into the keeping of the Victoria and Albert Museum in London. One depicts Jesus charging Peter to tend his sheep.

Raphael's masterpiece has been admired for many reasons: its keen sense of drama, its pioneering use of gestures and facial expressions to portray emotion, and the intricate detail of the landscape against which the action takes place (note, for example, the barn on fire slightly to the right of centre). Raphael places Peter at the core of the action and Christ to the left. (Raphael is, of course, forced to locate Christ on the left of the picture, in that Christ's left hand is outstretched in a gesture of acceptance and welcome to Peter.) The other ten are gathered round, observers of (rather than participants in) the personal drama being enacted before them.

With one finger, Christ points towards Peter; with another, towards the sheep. Raphael's imagery shows Christ as the connection between pastor and flock, the shared basis of their faith and their lives. In both his hands, Peter clasps a key – a symbol of spiritual authority. Raphael interprets the scene in terms of the personal recommissioning of Peter and his receipt of authority. To emphasize that it is the *risen* Christ commissioning Peter in this way, Raphael carefully places beneath Jesus' feet the stump of a tree surrounded by verdant growth. The stump is here a symbol of the cross seen from the standpoint of the resurrection. The power of the tree of death has been broken and replaced with the power to bring new life to nature and to broken humanity.

Yet the events of the High Priest's courtyard have not been forgotten. Scarcely has Peter been entrusted with his new responsibilities, than the theme of suffering returns once more. Christ explains to Peter that he must go to a place that is not of his own choosing, where his arms will be outstretched. (John adds a parenthetic note here: 'He said this to indicate the kind of death by which he would glorify God' (John 21.19).) As the long-standing tradition of Peter's martyrdom by crucifixion in Rome in AD 64 reminds us, Peter would not let Jesus down again.

Peter's public failure is thus redeemed through his reaffirmation by the risen Christ. He is restored in the sight of those who witnessed his earlier personal catastrophe; the door is thrown wide open to the renewal of his apostolic ministry within the Church. The one who called him has called him again, empowering and giving him authority (two themes linked with the gift of the Spirit). Yet it is important to note the introduction of a new factor into the situation. Previously, Peter had believed that he was perfectly prepared to die for Christ. Yet the resurrection of Christ pointed unequivocally to the resurrection of believers. As Peter later pointed out, in his mercy God had 'given us a new birth into a living hope through the resurrection of Jesus Christ from the dead' (1 Peter 1.3). The proclamation of the resurrection brings with it a re-evaluation of the place of life itself. Something greater still lies beyond it, forcing us to reappraise how much we value earthly existence and the priorities of life.

Lord, help us to know ourselves as you know us. Help us to identify our strengths and our weaknesses, and to put them both to service for you.

the road to Damascus

5 the road to Damascus

The resurrection of Jesus of Nazareth was an historical episode; it is, however, rather more than that. Thus far, we have concentrated on the events of the resurrection, and their revolutionary impact on some of the first Christians. But what about its significance for the way we understand reality? What difference does it make to our ideas? As the New Testament makes clear, the resurrection is crucial for any attempt to make sense of the identity of Jesus or to understand the purpose and place of humanity.

One of the major themes of the resurrection is the universal accessibility of the risen Christ. His power to transform and capacity to encounter humanity are no longer limited by geography, history or culture. The resurrected Christ transcends all boundaries. The famous episode involving Saul of Tarsus (later known as Paul), as he journeyed from Jerusalem to Damascus, is one of the most dramatic demonstrations of Jesus' ability to meet those who never knew him 'according to the flesh'. It is an incident of pivotal importance to the development of the early Christian Church and its understanding of the resurrection.

Scholarly attempts to reconstruct the early career of Saul have been generally unpersuasive. The New Testament indicates that he was a Jew who went on to become a Pharisee and was involved in early Jewish attempts to suppress Christianity. We know that he was born at Tarsus in Cilicia (Acts 21.39), and that he and his father were Roman citizens (Acts 22.26–28). His family appears to have been religiously observant (2 Timothy 1.3) and favoured Pharisaic traditions (Philippians 3.5–6). It is very difficult to date his career with any certainty, and that includes the famous journey to Damascus.

We possess four accounts of this iconic journey, each offering a narrative aimed at a different audience. Three are found in the Acts of the Apostles. The first of these (9.1–19) is narrated by the author himself; the second two (22.4–16; 26.9–19) form the core of Paul's self-defence before

Jews in Jerusalem and King Agrippa respectively. A fourth account is found in what is widely regarded as Paul's earliest writing to have survived – the letter to the Galatians (Galatians 1.11–24). Here, the account emphasizes Paul's independence from the other apostles, all of whom knew Jesus of Nazareth during his lifetime.

So what happened on the road to Damascus? The heart of the narrative concerns an encounter between Saul of Tarsus and the risen Christ. While journeying with an escort to the city of Damascus to search for and arrest Christians, Saul experienced a moment of devastating illumination: 'A light from heaven flashed around him' (Acts 9.3), leading to his being thrown to the ground and blinded. Many scholars have argued that this points to a moment of divine epiphany in which the overwhelming glory of God was temporarily revealed, with dramatic effect. Others have seen a connection with Deuteronomy 28.28–29, which speaks of the need for personal transformation and renewal, and which uses imagery that can be discerned in this famous story.

The emphasis on light immediately recalls the Genesis creation account, with its dramatic declaration: 'Let there be light.' Do we see here an anticipation of Paul's famous assertion that 'if anyone is in Christ, there is a new creation' (2 Corinthians 5.17)? The New Testament often uses the language of 'being born again' or 'being made new' to describe the difference made by an encounter with Christ. Paul's language is still more dramatic, seeing a person's transformation through Christ as an extension of the work of creation itself.

The moment is captured in a seventeenth-century illustration, based on a famous earlier work of Peter Paul Rubens, which depicts Saul thrown to the ground while above him the heavens are parted in a moment of revelation. This overwhelming disclosure of the glory of the risen Christ is

accompanied by a voice speaking: 'Saul, Saul, why do you persecute me?' Astonished, Saul asks the speaker to name himself. The reply is of central importance to any attempt to appreciate the significance of the resurrection: 'I am Jesus, whom you are persecuting.' From our perspective, we see Saul sprawled helpless on the ground; from Saul's perspective, he sees the risen Christ, who alone has the power to raise him up – not just physically, from the ground, but spiritually, from his entrapment to sin (a major theme in Romans 7.15–25).

The artist shows Saul spreadeagled on the ground. As we look more closely, we realize the significance of this: Saul is being portrayed as if he were crucified. So what are we to read into this remarkable visual echo of the crucifixion of Christ? The most persuasive answer lies in one of Paul's great theological insights – that coming to Christ is about being crucified with Christ and dying to one's old self: 'I have been crucified with Christ; and it is no longer I who live, but it is Christ who lives in me' (Galatians 2.19–20). The encounter with the risen Christ leads to the death of Saul the zealous persecutor of the Church, and the birth of Paul the apostle to the Gentiles.

At one level, the story can be read as an affirmation of the wisdom of God. It is tempting to believe that the Christians in Damascus were earnestly praying that they might be delivered from persecution. God's response was not to remove or neutralize their persecutor, but to transform him utterly. The same pattern of encounter and change found in the gospel resurrection narratives is played out all over again. There are differences – important differences. The most significant is that Paul never knew Jesus of Nazareth during his earthly ministry. Yet this proved no barrier to his meeting Christ and being commissioned by him to act as an apostle.

So what is going on here? Traditionally, this episode is described as a 'conversion'. There is undoubtedly truth in this – Paul was changed dramatically from being the Church's main persecutor to being one of its most important advocates in the Gentile world. At another level, it is helpful to see this as a 'calling', similar to that of Samuel or any other of the great Old Testament prophets. We see hints of this idea in Paul's letters, in which we read the claim that he was set apart before he was born and called through grace, not by 'any human being' (Galatians 1.15–16), for a mission to the Gentiles. Paul was often to appeal to his encounter with the risen Christ as the ultimate validation of his ministry.

At one level, then, the conversion or calling of Paul is a direct outcome of the removal of all spatial and chronological limitations to the scope of Christ's action in the world. Paul's experience has served as a model for countless others who have had similar experiences down the centuries. It can be seen as the prototype for personal narratives of encounter between believers and the risen Christ. Yet Paul's experience went beyond his own volte-face; it also led to a major revision in his way of conceiving God's dealings with the world and, above all, with the Gentiles. So important is this point that we need to explore it a little further.

For Paul, the resurrection clinched the arguments for Christ's being the long-awaited Messiah, the one who would fulfil the hopes and aspirations of Israel. Jesus was 'was descended from David according to the flesh and was declared to be Son of God with power according to the spirit of holiness by resurrection from the dead' (Romans 1.3–4). In other words, any human judgement that Jesus of Nazareth was the Messiah, based on his legal descent, was dramatically and conclusively endorsed by the divine action of resurrection. God, by raising Jesus from the dead, had proclaimed that he was indeed the true Messiah, the culmination and fulfilment of Israel's law and destiny. He was undoubtedly the 'son of God' in the Davidic sense that we find in such great anticipatory texts as 2 Samuel 7 or Psalm 2.

The sections of Paul's letters dealing with circumcision, often skipped over by modern readers who regard them as having little relevance to today's debates, reflect a passionate conviction that the resurrection of Christ changed the rules of engagement. No longer was physical birth as a Jew a mark of spiritual privilege. No longer was the observance of the Jewish religious law the precondition for salvation or a mark of belonging to the people of God. All could be 'sons of God', through the new order (which Christians quickly began to describe as a 'new covenant') that God had established through the resurrection. Whereas Israel tended to think of the Gentiles as being permitted access to their God grudgingly, and only to a limited extent, Paul insisted that Gentiles were accepted by God on the same terms. Jews and Gentiles would have equal status within the Church and in the sight of God.

Paul's experience on the road to Damascus made it clear that the covenant God of Israel was to be experienced outside the geographical boundaries of the land of Israel and apart from its cultic institutions. If the resurrection of Christ was an act of the same God who had guided and commissioned Israel throughout its long history, then a major new phase in the history of the people of God had begun. The resurrection of Christ redefined the identity of Israel. Although some have suggested that hints

of anti-Semitism can be discerned in these ideas, it is clear that Paul's concern was to redefine the people of Israel. In much the same way as an Old Testament prophet, Paul wanted the purification and renewal of Israel, taking full account of the dramatic intervention of Israel's God in the life, death and resurrection of Jesus of Nazareth (who was himself, of course, a Jew).

One of the central themes we have considered in this chapter is 'resurrection as re-creation'. Although we have been focusing on Paul's reflections on the implications of this event for the faith and identity of Israel, the theme also has wider ramifications. It speaks of a God who is able to renew all things, even when they seem to be dead and beyond any hope of restoration. It is a theme that regularly surfaces in church history, when the institution of the Church seems moribund and its future uncertain. The dramatic rise of Pentecostalism in the twentieth century is seen by many as a judgement on the failings of traditional forms of Christianity, and an affirmation of God's capacity to do new things in the life of his people and institutions.

Yet for many, the most important aspect of the resurrection lies at the personal level. It is about the hope of transformation in the face of personal weakness, failure, sin and despair. What hope is there for any of us, many wonder, when we seem incapable of confronting, let alone curbing, our personal demons? These thoughts trouble many, as they are known to have troubled the noted Victorian poet Christina Rossetti (1830–94). Rossetti lived out what many regarded as a deeply unhappy life, based on hope rather than actuality, faith rather than substance. In her moving poem 'A better resurrection', she reflected, in a dark and sombre mood, on the futility and pointlessness of life without the hope of transformation – a transformation that could take place only through the work of the God who raised the dead.

I have no wit, no words, no tears;
My heart within me like a stone
Is numbed too much for hopes or fears.
Look right, look left, I dwell alone;
I lift mine eyes, but dimmed with grief
No everlasting hills I see;
My life is in the falling leaf:
O Jesus, quicken me.

My life is like a faded leaf,
My harvest dwindled to a husk:
Truly my life is void and brief
And tedious in the barren dusk;
My life is like a frozen thing,
No bud nor greenness can I see:
Yet rise it shall – the sap of spring;
O Jesus, rise in me.

My life is like a broken bowl,
A broken bowl that cannot hold
One drop of water for my soul
Or cordial in the searching cold;
Cast in the fire the perished thing;
Melt and remould it, till it be
A royal cup for Him, my King:
O Jesus, drink of me.

The poem speaks of powerlessness, decay and mortality, and the threat that they pose to meaningful human existence. Rossetti was clear that she could not hope to break their power nor undo their damage, whether through her own resources or through anything that nature could offer. The hope of resurrection kept her going during these times of despair and despondency. As she contemplated the challenges of life (note the allusion in the 'everlasting hills' to Psalm 121), she affirmed that the proclamation of the resurrection of Christ had the power to revitalize and reanimate her, and enable her to live her life to the full.

Lord, may we know you as the one who can renew our faded leaves with your sap of spring. Melt and remould us in the fires of your love so that we may serve you and proclaim you as you deserve.

the fulfilment of prophecy

6 the fulfilment of prophecy

The New Testament leaves us in no doubt that the resurrection is a drama – not simply something unexpected and breathtaking, but something that takes place within a theatrical context. The Christian tradition has long thought of the spheres of history and nature as the 'theatre of the glory of God' (John Calvin). God directs the great drama of salvation, which Christian theology has often divided into 'acts', such as the calling of Abraham, the exodus from Egypt, the coming of Jesus Christ, the age of the Church, and the final hope of resurrection and renewal in Christ.

To begin with, the first Christians focused on the realization that he who had been crucified was restored to them. He had commissioned them again to proclaim the gospel to the ends of the earth, promising to be with them for ever (Matthew 28.18–20). Yet the question of what the resurrection *meant* could not be sidestepped or postponed indefinitely. At one level, we find an insistence that the resurrection demonstrated that the crucifixion was not a defeat. Neither did Christ's death on a cross indicate that (as a strict reading of parts of the Old Testament might suggest) he died under a divine curse. The resurrection was about the vindication of Christ and his elevation to God's right hand.

In both the Pauline epistles and the early chapters of the Acts of the Apostles, the early Church's beliefs about the resurrection's significance were set out in terms of the exaltation of Jesus. The resurrection demonstrated that Jesus of Nazareth was Lord, Messiah, Saviour and Son of God. Many great themes of the Old Testament were believed to have been fulfilled in this event. A classic example is Psalm 2, which speaks of the enthronement of the 'son of God': 'You are my son: today I have begotten you' (Psalm 2.7). The resurrection of Jesus was interpreted as his enthronement in heaven. In a Davidic context, this could be considered to be his royal coronation and thus a demonstration that he had been begotten as the Son of God.

The resurrection thus transformed an understanding of who Jesus of Nazareth was. The hints of his true identity in the Gospels – such as his claim to be able to forgive sins (something that only God was meant to be able to do) – were seen in a new light. The resurrection could be thought of as a retrospective confirmation of the identity of Jesus as the Son of God, already partially disclosed (for those who had eyes to see) in the gospel narratives themselves. Yet if Jesus was indeed the Messianic 'Son of God', it followed that those who shared the 'sonship' of the Messiah would share as well the 'inheritance' that is promised in Psalm 2. This central theme was affirmed by Paul, who spoke of the importance of the gift of the Spirit in confirming our adoption as children of God and hence as inheritors of the promises of God.

> When we cry, 'Abba! Father!', it is that very Spirit bearing witness with our spirit that we are children of God, and if children, then heirs, heirs of God and joint heirs with Christ – if, in fact, we suffer with him so that we may also be glorified with him (Romans 8.15b–17).

The fact that Jesus was raised not as a disembodied spirit but as a physical, corporeal entity was clearly of great significance to New Testament writers. Here we see a fundamental affirmation of the continuity between the old and the new, with important implications for our understanding of our own resurrection. Yes, we shall be changed, as a seed is utterly transformed into a full-grown plant, yet there is continuity between those two forms. In some way, there is a real connection between the life we are now living and its radical transformation through the resurrection.

How are we to understand this? A favourite image of some early Christian writers was to think of the resurrection of the body as a disfigured

metal statue that was recast. Methodius of Olympus (died *c.* 311) asked his readers to imagine that the same craftsman, who had made the original statue in all its beauty and glory, melted it down and recast it, with all its blemishes and defects removed and all the damage repaired. This process of recasting affirmed the continuity between the old and the new, while insisting upon the transformation brought about by the resurrection. The hope of the resurrection was thus linked with renewal: 'See, I am making all things new' (Revelation 21.5). Our physical bodies may be ravaged and disfigured by age, sin and illness but we live in the hope of our renewal and transformation.

This theme was expressed visually in what many regard as one of the finest pieces of art of the early sixteenth century – the Isenheim altarpiece by Matthias Grünewald (*c.* 1475–1528). Around the year 1515, Grünewald was commissioned to produce an altarpiece for the hospital chapel of Saint Anthony's Monastery at Isenheim, about twenty miles south of Colmar in Alsace. The hospital specialized in the treatment of skin diseases, such as leprosy, which often caused terrible disfigurement to those affected by them. The central panel depicts the crucifixion in a dramatic manner, portraying Christ as emaciated, pock-marked and discoloured. As we look more closely, we see that the thorns of the scourges are embedded in the festering wounds that cover the whole of Christ's body. His dark red blood is contrasted with the sickly green of the flesh, clearly intended to represent a serious illness. Christ is thus portrayed as 'a man of suffering and acquainted with infirmity . . . [who] has borne our infirmities and carried our diseases' (Isaiah 53.3–4). The theological message is unambiguous: this is the one who bears your afflictions and is your ultimate hope of renewal.

Yet one of the altarpiece's side-panels, which deals with the resurrection of Christ, is too easily overlooked on account of the dramatic power of the central illustration. At first sight, Grünewald's representation of the resurrection seems totally surreal. It seems as if Christ is simply soaring out of his grave, surrounded by an unearthly, eerie light. The sheer drama of the resurrection is captured in the helpless, pointless gestures of the soldiers on the ground. They are simply dazzled and overwhelmed by this sudden bright apparition, which leaves them utterly powerless to resist what is happening. Their faces are averted from the luminosity of the rising Christ; this might be a human reaction to an unexpected display of brilliance but it is more likely intended to emphasize the inability of the world to grasp, entrap and hold down the risen Christ: 'The light shines in the darkness, and the darkness did not overcome it' (John 1.5).

Then our eyes turn to examine the figure of the rising Christ. We can hardly overlook the pictorial emphasis that Grünewald has placed on the *stigmata* – the gaping nail holes in Christ's hands and feet and the spear wound in his side. The point is clear: the one who is rising is none other than the one who was crucified. Anticipating a contemporary Doubting Thomas, Grünewald reminds us of that seminal scene in John's Gospel considered earlier (pages 33–4). Yet that is not the main point he wishes to make. As we look more closely, we suddenly realize that the blemishes, bruises and deformities of the crucified Christ have vanished. The hope of healing and renewal has been reaffirmed. Christ has indeed borne our infirmities and diseases; yet they have been taken away, not taken elsewhere.

At several points in the writings of Paul, the theme of resurrection is linked with the renewal of all creation. For example, 1 Corinthians 15.20–28 sets out an explicitly Messianic theology in which Jesus, as the Son of God, is proclaimed the agent of God as creator and 're-creator'. He accomplishes precisely this task of purging God's creation of evil and death. The resurrection of Christ is thus a tangible pledge that the whole creation will finally shake off its corruption and decay as God extends his work of regeneration. There is a world that is to come in which death itself – the ultimate sign and consequence of sin, disorder and decay – will ultimately be abolished. Until that day, creation groans, waiting for its final renewal (Romans 8.19–23).

We should pause at this point and note that there is an explicitly political element to the resurrection of Christ, one easily overlooked by those with privatized or pietist understandings of the nature of faith. Studies of the first-century Graeco-Roman world have highlighted the quasi-religious role played by the Roman state and its institutions, particularly the imperial cult and its associated ideology. The Roman Empire had a religious basis: indeed, the Latin word *religio* is probably derived from the root term meaning 'tying or binding together'. Worship of the emperor was seen as an essentialway of binding together a loose association of subservient states into a coherent unity.

The first Christians proclaimed a message that was profoundly subversive in this imperial context. Through the resurrection, they argued, God had designated and enthroned the true king of the world. When Paul wrote 'we are ambassadors for Christ' (2 Corinthians 5.20), he was articulating a message that could only be construed as deeply counter-

imperial, as subversive to the whole edifice of the Roman Empire at that time. Believers were representatives of another king and another kingdom – one that challenged the values and ultimately undermined the existence of the *imperium Romanum*.

Paul's vision of the gospel of Christ affirms that Christians submit themselves to Christ as Lord, accepting no alternatives (secular or religious). At the same time, there is the insistence that this message be proclaimed to the nations in anticipation of a response. The world is thus invited to be loyal to this new king, to order its life according to his story, his symbols and his praxis, and to conform its mind according to his truth: 'Our citizenship is in heaven, and it is from there that we are expecting a Saviour, the Lord Jesus Christ' (Philippians 3.20). In every respect, this represented a powerful challenge to the prevailing ideology of power.

Although the themes of renewal and transformation play a highly important role in the New Testament's understanding of the meaning of the resurrection, there are others that deserve to be noted. One of these is the idea of victory. The resurrection of Christ represents the victory of God over forces of disorder, decay and corruption – within humanity and in society. The 'principalities and powers' that govern this universe (and Paul clearly has in mind spiritual, as much as political, forces) have been given notice that they are on their way out. Their claims to authority have been neutralized and their actual grip on power has been terminally weakened because of what God has done through Christ (Ephesians 6.10–13).

We also need to remember here that Paul is emphatic that there is only one God – the covenant God of Israel, who has raised Christ from the dead and ushered in a new era in the history of his people. Paul does not for one moment believe that these 'powers' are really alternative gods. The problem is that they are treated as such by humans, who choose to treat aspects of God's creation as if they are divine and worthy of worship. The resurrection of Christ breaks their power, partly by exposing them as subordinate to the one and only true God, the ruler of all the world.

The victory in question is not immediate, however, as if death, sin and other oppressive forces are neutralized and swept away from the sphere of human existence. Rather, we are able to face them, knowing that their malign influence is broken. Like an illness that is being cured or an enemy in retreat, death and sin are vacating the premises. They need no longer be feared: the one who is stronger than they has made his presence and power known to us. Death itself shall die!

This is the leading theme of what some view as John Donne's most profound 'divine meditation', published in 1633. Although Donne makes no explicit reference to God or to the resurrection of Christ, the language and imagery of 1 Corinthians 15 (especially verses 26, 54–57) is evident.

> Death, be not proud, though some have called thee
> Mighty and dreadful, for thou art not so;
> For those whom thou thinkst thou dost overthrow,

Die not, poor Death, nor yet canst thou kill me.
From rest and sleep, which but thy pictures be,
Much pleasure – then, from thee much more must flow;
And soonest our best men with thee do go,
Rest of their bones and soul's delivery.
Thou'rt slave to fate, chance, kings, and desperate men,
And dost with poison, war, and sickness dwell;
And poppy or charms can make us sleep as well
And better than thy stroke. Why swellst thou then?
One short sleep past, we wake eternally,
And death shall be no more. Death, thou shalt die.
('Holy Sonnets' iii)

Lord, help us to live this life in the hope of the life to come, not neglecting things around us but seeing them in a new way.

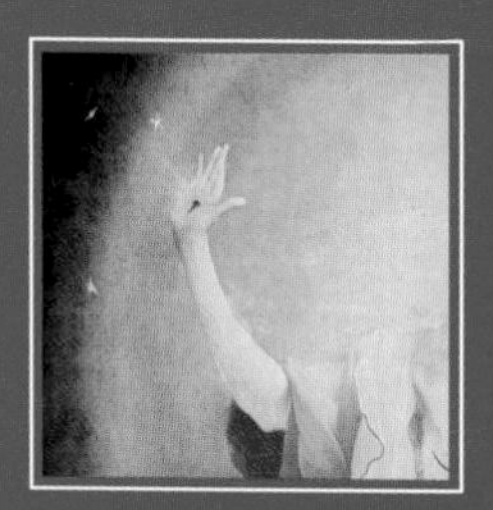

making all things new

7 making all things new

At times, the Christian faith makes an appeal to our longing to make sense of things. Who are we? Why are we here? Why is there anything here – including ourselves – at all? And, as we have seen, the resurrection is one more piece in the theological jigsaw that discloses the true identity of Jesus of Nazareth, the nature and purposes of God and the nature of heaven.

Yet the idea of heaven is notoriously resistant to conceptual analysis. It is something that calls out to be visualized in our mind's eye, rather than dissected by reason. It is no accident that the New Testament book that deals with the topic of heaven at greatest length – the Revelation to St John (sometimes known as the 'Apocalypse') – is heavily based on images. We are invited to *imagine* what heaven is like. The New Jerusalem is one of the most famous of these images.

The city of Jerusalem is seen by the Old Testament writers as a tangible symbol of the presence and providence of God within its sturdy walls and also as a pointer to the fulfilment of Messianic expectations. The New Testament develops this theme, especially in the book of Revelation. For John, all Christian hopes and expectations converge on the New Jerusalem, the city of God within which the risen Christ reigns triumphant.

> I saw the holy city, the new Jerusalem, coming down out of heaven from God, prepared as a bride adorned for her husband. And I heard a loud voice from the throne saying, 'See, the home of God is among mortals. He will dwell with them; they will be his peoples, and God himself will be with them; he will wipe every tear from their eyes. Death will be no more; mourning and crying and pain will be no more, for the first things have passed away.' And the one who was seated on the throne said, 'See, I am making all things new.' (Revelation 21.2–5)

The imagery is powerful and at times challenging to our preconceptions. (We naturally think in terms of our own ascent to heaven; the passage actually speaks of the New Jerusalem coming down to humanity, almost as an extension of the incarnation.)

Why is this image of the New Jerusalem so powerful? What ideas does it convey? The theme of the New Jerusalem is integrated with motifs drawn from the creation account, such as the presence of the 'tree of life' (Revelation 22.2). These suggest that heaven can be seen as the restoration of the bliss of Eden, when God dwelt with humanity in harmony. In John's vision, the pain, sorrow and evil of a fallen world have finally passed away, and creation is restored to its original intention.

When John was writing, the Christians of Asia Minor were few in number and generally of low social status. They would have derived much consolation (as we may also) from the anticipation of entering a heavenly metropolis that vastly exceeded any earthly comforts or security they had known. The holy city was paved with gold and decked with jewels and precious stones, dazzling its inhabitants. Contemplation of this city would have intensified the longing of those still on earth to enter through its gates.

The New Jerusalem – like its earthly counterpart – is portrayed as being walled, a place of safety and security. The twelve gates of the New Jerusalem, although guarded by angels, are permanently thrown open. Whereas the classic fortified city of ancient times was designed to exclude outsiders, the architecture of the New Jerusalem seems intended to welcome them within its boundaries. The city is portrayed as a mathematically accurate cube (Revelation 21.16). It perhaps signified a perfect example of the square temple that the prophet Ezekiel envisaged for Jerusalem after the Jews' return from Babylonian exile (Ezekiel 48.20).

Most significantly of all, the New Jerusalem does not contain a temple (21.22). The cultic hierarchies of the old priestly tradition are swept to one side. All believers are priests, and there is no need for a temple because God dwells within the city as a whole. Where Old Testament prophets had yearned for the rebuilding of the temple, Revelation declares that it has become redundant. What the temple foreshadowed has now taken place: with the advent of the reality of God's presence, its symbol is no longer required. God now dwells with his people. The New Jerusalem is thus characterized by the pervasive presence of God, and the triumphant and joyful response of those who have long awaited this experience.

In his classic vision, Bernard of Cluny (*c.* 1100 – *c.* 1150) vividly depicts the heavenly city in evocative terms designed to captivate the imagination and galvanize the human longing to enter its portals. The New Jerusalem exceeds in beauty and glory anything that the human heart can desire and hope to embrace.

> Jerusalem the golden,
> With milk and honey blessed,
> Beneath thy contemplation
> Sink heart and voice oppressed.
> I know not, O, I know not
> What joys await us there,
> What radiancy of glory,
> What bliss beyond compare.
>
> O sweet and blessed country,
> The home of God's elect!
> O sweet and blessed country

That eager hearts expect!
Jesu, in mercy bring us
To that dear land of rest;
Who art, with God the Father,
And Spirit, ever blessed.

Bernard here sets out a vision of the wondrous place that lies ahead as a means of encouraging and sustaining Christian faith in the present, stressing the inability of human language to convey adequately the wonders of heaven (the human voice is thus 'oppressed'). Believers, he insists, can be assured that all these wonderful things are awaiting them. They can anticipate entering through the gates and sharing in the city's delights. Those who find the life of faith wearying and dispiriting can thus take comfort and encouragement from this vision of the New Jerusalem, and keep going on the road that leads to the celestial city.

Yet the book of Revelation interweaves other images of heaven with that of the New Jerusalem. One of these is of the restoration of Eden, inviting us to think of heaven as a renewed paradise. While it is customary to speak of the 'Garden of Eden', it is perhaps better to think of 'Eden' as the region in which the garden is located, rather than the name of the garden itself. Other biblical passages designate the garden in alternative ways – such as the 'garden of God' (Ezekiel 28.13) or the 'garden of the LORD' (Isaiah 51.3). The garden rapidly became a symbol of innocence and harmony, a place of peace, rest and fertility. The powerful imagery of the four rivers that permanently watered the rich ground, and its opulent plant and animal life, served as a stimulus to the imaginations of Christian writers.

'Paradise' (originally a Persian word) came to be imbued with a series of qualities that ensured its place as a core theme in the Christian account of heaven. Paradise was seen, like the Garden of Eden, as a place of fertility and harmony, where humanity dwelt in peace with nature and 'walked with God'. That idyllic state had been lost at the dawn of history, with our expulsion from paradise. The hope of restoration of this paradisiacal relationship was (and is) an integral aspect of any Christian account of the consequences of the resurrection of Christ.

A central element of the restored paradise of heaven, as seen in the book of Revelation, is 'the river of the water of life', which flows from the throne of God (Revelation 21.1–2). On either side of the river is the 'tree of life', the leaves of which are 'for the healing of the nations'. The parallels with the Garden of Eden are clear and immensely significant. William Blake's famous watercolour of 1805, entitled *The River of Life*, represents a highly imaginative rendering of this theme. The river cleanses souls of their dirt and stains, and satisfies the thirst of those who are parched. The trees by its side offer healing to the soul. Heaven is a restored paradise in which the thirsty find refreshment, the sick healing and the exhausted rest.

For Paul, part of the inheritance for believers of Christ's resurrection is that they are 'citizens of heaven' (Philippians 3.20), who share in the life of heaven in the present. Roman citizens serving abroad had the right to return and live in the great city of Rome. In the same way, Christians, although

living on earth, share in the worship of heaven, observe its laws and eagerly anticipate their return to their homeland. It is a theme familiar to many through the great medieval hymn of Peter Abelard (1079–1142), who likens our time on earth to the people of Jerusalem's long exile in Babylon:

> Now, in the meanwhile, with hearts raised on high,
> We for that country must yearn and must sigh,
> Seeking Jerusalem, dear native land,
> Through our long exile on Babylon's strand.

One of the great themes of Christian spirituality is the idea of finally entering heaven and seeing God face to face (1 Corinthians 13.12). The Psalmist set out his longing to see God in Psalm 27:

> One thing I asked of the LORD,
> that will I seek after:
> to live in the house of the LORD
> all the days of my life,
> to behold the beauty of the LORD.

The Christian vision of heaven affirms that what the Psalmist longed for will one day be the common privilege of all the people of God – to gaze upon the face of their Lord and Saviour, as they dwell in peace with him for ever. As John Donne once put it: 'No man ever saw God and lived. And yet, I shall not live till I see God; and when I have seen him, I shall never die.'

In his 'Prayer to Christ', Anselm of Canterbury (*c.* 1033–1109) sets out his longing to be with Christ in heaven. It is a desire that heightens his sense of sadness at not yet seeing the glorious face of Christ, while offering him hope and encouragement that one day his exile will be over. Again, the image of exile shapes and informs his thought:

> I weep over the hardship of exile,
> Hoping in the sole consolation of your coming,
> Ardently longing for the glorious contemplation of your face.

Similar themes can be found in the poetry of Henry Vaughan (1622–95), who appears to have undergone some kind of spiritual conversion in response to personal difficulties and hardship. He later remarked that 'certain divine rays break out of the soul in adversity, like sparks out of the afflicted flint'. Perhaps it should not be surprising that the theme of heaven played a major role in Vaughan's spirituality, evident especially in his poem 'Peace'. Writing in the aftermath of the English Civil War, which had shattered the political and social orders of his day, Vaughan spoke of the soul's only hope for true peace lying in 'a country far beyond the stars'.

> If thou canst get but thither,
> There grows the flower of Peace,
> The Rose that cannot wither,
> Thy fortress, and thy ease.

Leave then thy foolish ranges,
For none can thee secure
But one who never changes,
Thy God, thy life, thy cure.

Some have suggested that belief in the resurrection is about escapism, that it is a futile and pointless attempt to run away from the realities of life and find solace in a fantasy world. Nothing in the New Testament lends any support to this idea. The resurrection does not mandate Christians to avoid engaging with this world or to ignore its sorrows and pains. We are called upon to work to make this world a better place, anticipating the liberty and righteousness of the New Jerusalem.

Yet we cannot help but see this world in a new light. It no longer defines the horizons of human existence. It is no longer the goal of human longing or achievement. It has been transcended. We are called to live life to the full while knowing that something still better awaits us. The old Prayer Book collect for Ascension Day expresses this perfectly, in a prayer ideally suited to bringing this short book to a close:

Grant, we beseech thee, Almighty God, that like as we do believe thy only-begotten Son our Lord Jesus Christ to have ascended into the heavens; so we may also in heart and mind thither ascend, and with him continually dwell, who liveth and reigneth with thee and the Holy Ghost, one God, world without end. Amen.

for further reading

Introductory

Brown, Raymond E., *A Risen Christ at Eastertime.* Collegeville, Minn.: Liturgical Press, 1991.

Davis, Stephen T., O'Collins, Gerald and Kendall, Daniel (eds), *The Resurrection: An Interdisciplinary Symposium on the Resurrection of Jesus.* Oxford: Oxford University Press, 1998.

O'Collins, Gerald, *Jesus Risen: An Historical, Fundamental and Systematic Examination of Christ's Resurrection.* New York, NY: Paulist Press, 1987.

Ramsey, Arthur Michael, *The Resurrection of Christ.* London: Collins, 1961.

More advanced

Becker, Jürgen, *Paul: Apostle to the Gentiles.* Louisville, Ky.: Westminster John Knox Press, 1993.

Bynum, Caroline Walker, *The Resurrection of the Body in Western Christianity, 200–1336.* New York, NY: Columbia University Press, 1995.

Davis, Stephen T., *Risen Indeed: Making Sense of the Resurrection.* Grand Rapids, Mich.: Eerdmans, 1993.

Donaldson, Terence L., *Paul and the Gentiles: Remapping the Apostle's Convictional World.* Minneapolis, Minn.: Fortress Press, 1997.

Fishwick, Duncan, *The Imperial Cult in the Latin West: Studies in the Ruler Cult of the Western Provinces of the Roman Empire.* Leiden: E. J. Brill, 2005.

Horsley, Richard A. *Paul and Empire: Religion and Power in Roman Imperial Society.* Harrisburg, Penn.: Trinity Press International, 1997.

Lincoln, Andrew T., *Paradise Now and Not Yet: Studies in the Role of the Heavenly Dimension in Paul's Thought with Special Reference to His Eschatology.* Cambridge: Cambridge University Press, 1981.

McDannell, Colleen and Lang, Bernhard, *Heaven: A History.* New Haven, Conn.: Yale University Press, 1988.

McKnight, Scot, *Turning to Jesus: The Sociology of Conversion in the Gospels.* Louisville, Ky.: Westminster John Knox Press, 2002.

O'Donovan, Oliver, *Resurrection and Moral Order.* Grand Rapids, Mich.: Eerdmans, 1986.

Perkins, Pheme, *Resurrection: New Testament Witness and Contemporary Reflection.* Garden City, NY: Doubleday, 1984.

Peters, Ted, Robert, J. Russell and Welker, Michael (eds), *Resurrection: Theological and Scientific Assessments.* Grand Rapids, Mich.: Eerdmans, 2002.

Ratzinger, Joseph, *Eschatology.* Washington, DC: Catholic University of America Press, 1989.

Reiser, Marius, *Jesus and Judgment: The Eschatological Proclamation in its Jewish Context.* Minneapolis, Minn.: Fortress Press, 1997.

Russell, Jeffrey Burton, *A History of Heaven: The Singing Silence.* Princeton, NJ: Princeton University Press, 1997.

Stanley, David Michael, *Christ's Resurrection in Pauline Soteriology.* Rome: Pontifical Biblical Institute, 1961.

Stewart, Robert B., *The Resurrection of Jesus: John Dominic Crossan and N. T. Wright in Dialogue.* London: SPCK, 2006.

Swinburne, Richard, *The Resurrection of God Incarnate.* Oxford: Clarendon Press, 2003.

Torrance, Thomas F., *Space, Time and Resurrection.* Edinburgh: Handsel Press, 1976.

Wedderburn, A. J. M., *Baptism and Resurrection: Studies in Pauline Theology against its Graeco-Roman Background.* Tübingen: J. C. B. Mohr, 1987.

Williams, Rowan, *Resurrection: Interpreting the Easter Gospel*, 2nd edn. London: Darton, Longman & Todd, 2002.

Wright, N. T., *The Resurrection of the Son of God.* London: SPCK, 2003.

illustrations

Holy Women at the Tomb, 1894 (oil on canvas), by Maurice Denis (1870–1943), Musée Maurice Denis, St Germain-en-Laye, France, Lauros/Giraudon/The Bridgeman Art Library, © ADAGP, Paris and DACS, London 2006.

On the Road to Emmaus, 1978, by He Qi, China.

The Incredulity of St Thomas (oil on canvas) by Guercino (Giovanni Francesco Barbieri, 1591–1666), Vatican, Pinacoteca, © 1990, Photo Scala, Florence.

Christ's Charge to St Peter (cartoon for the Sistine Chapel, pre-restoration) by Raphael (Raffaello Sanzio of Urbino, 1483–1520), Victoria and Albert Museum, London, UK/The Bridgeman Art Library.

The Conversion of St Paul (oil on canvas) by Peter Paul Rubens (after, 1577–1640, Flemish), Christies Images/www.superstock.co.uk.

The Resurrection from the Isenheim Altarpiece, 1510–16 (oil on limewood), by Matthias Grünewald (*c.* 1475–1528), © Musée d'Unterlinden, Colmar, France, Photo O. Zimmermann.

The River of Life, c. 1805 (pen and ink and watercolour on paper), by William Blake (1757–1827), © Tate, London 2006.